A WARM WELCOME
FROM THE AUTHOR TO
ALL MY PEOPLE OF
AWEHNESS

REJECTED CHAPPIES FACTS

## PREFACE

Rejected Chappies Facts began as a 'Literary Arts' project on Social Media by the Author 'Rejected Chappie'. It's debut was successful, but there was something more special behind the writing: a unique Mind attempting to resonate with fellow thinkers.

In the author's own words...

"Rejected Chappies Facts is a counter-response to the familiar Chappies Facts but with more reflective facts more useful to everyone on a personal level. My name is 'Rejected Chappie' & these are my facts..."

REJECTED CHAPPIES FACTS

## VOLUME 1

## THE FIRST COLLECTION

Did you know?
The power of enlightened literature is to put readers to silence... - knowing that the only closeness any of us have ever come to knowing our true selves was in nothing more than Pure Silence. This is one of the few gateways to true introspection & deep meditation. Another being 'The Art of Action' as sometimes a simple gesture can explain something ineffable.

Did you know?
If you, through moral weakness, encourage lies instead of honesty, a liar will then think it's okay & not only

continue but eventually graduate to
other forms of dishonesty - like theft.

Did you know?
There is a difference between receiving
& taking - receiving lies in honesty,
taking lies in lies.

Did you know?
If you publicly praise One thing that
created All things and nothing inferior,
but privately claim your own 'thing' to
be superior to others - that's called
'hypocrisy'...

Did you know?
There is a difference in acceptance &
encouragement, acceptance being a
stable understanding of both sides,
encouragement being temporary one-
sidedness.

REJECTED CHAPPIES FACTS

Did you know?
If you think twice before you act you will avoid second-guessing yourself.

Did you know?
If you are a skillful musician in the modern world & sacrifice time in front of your microphone or instrument for too much time in front of a camera or people (as many will encourage) - you will lose your musical skill for selfy &/or socialite 'skill'...

Did you know?
If all the forces continuously trying to stop you from being who you must and living your life is a metaphorical 'ocean of tides'... - you must first 'put your foot down' to 'stem the tide', & when you're done - walk the way you must.

Did you know?
The truth hurts & lies comfort because comfort is a lie & hurt is a Truth.

Did you know?
Bad news travels slow & good news travels fast - flip that around and you will be successful in your business.

Did you know?
An inner voice will always give you knowledge that cannot be propounded by the outside world.

Did you know?
The slowest but most certain object to win in a fight against a rock (or 'earth element') is the element - water... & yet the quickest and most certain object to win in a fight against water - is a rock (or the 'earth' element). One is quicker and one is slower yet eventually they are completely equal in strength.

REJECTED CHAPPIES FACTS

Did you know?
Nothing is what it seems.

Did you know?
Experience exceeds/surpasses age,
which is why younger people, who have
more experience in a matter, get
annoyed when older people condescend
them in ignorance.

Did you know?
When someone exclaims this question
to you - 'Who do you think you are!?'...
you can win the argument by
responding - 'Who do you think you are
to ask me who I think I am?'

Did you know?
If you are happy with nothing -
everything is a delight... & If you can

resist excessive indulgence you will live perfectly well no matter your income.

Did you know?
Most weaklings only dabble in armed combat their whole lives, but unarmed combat will always be your first and last method of physical defense. Therefor it will behoove you to train in the latter as a higher priority in terms of defense combat for yourself and your family in emergency situations.

Did you know?
The ancient Egyptians built pyramids by using huge stones of different sizes and shapes to build one perfectly proportional structure. The method is called 'heterogeneous building'... today we use small proportional stones of equal size and shape to build basic structures. Otherwise known as 'simple lazy shit'.

REJECTED CHAPPIES FACTS

Did you know?
The more you give the more is given to you, the more you take - the more is taken from you.

Did you know?
'First impressions last but last impressions remain' because the only constant in the Universe - is change...

Did you know?
Only through experience do we gain insights to emotional, physical & spiritual well-being which, when applied, this knowledge & understanding becomes Wisdom (as Wisdom is Applied Understanding in Action and not simply knowledge). Learning from experience is thus the only way to unshackle us from ignorance... and the most powerful guide in that endeavor - are feelings &

emotions. This is the One force, the lighthouse seen from oceans - to lead us home.

Did you know?
An understanding of 'The Fibonacci series', Advanced Algebra, the Golden Ratio, the Meter, the Speed of Light & Pi are all found within the shape, diameters and proportions of the Great Pyramid of Giza – which is part of 'the astronomical Clock of our planet', created by certain adept human beings well over 4500 years ago.

Did you know?
If a person, through ignorance, makes a mistake in life for the first time – it's not their fault… but if the person refuses to learn the lesson and then knowingly makes the same mistake, having been given the choice to rise above and do better for themselves and others, only

then have they truly faulted against themselves.

Did you know?
Although 'The Devil' was once 'The Angel of Music', after it's exile it never created music again... therefor music is still 'God's Territory' and not 'The Devils'.

Did you know?
A true Warrior will never start fights but will never hesitate to end them either.

Did you know?
A musical person gets annoyed by 'out-of-tune' talk and a dissonant person gets annoyed by perfectly harmonious music.

Did you know?
If you give something with the hidden intention of unfairly getting a lot more

out of it then you are not giving anything but are practicing a nuanced form of taking - known as 'con artistry'.

Did you know?
A master is someone who can deliver 'punches' to your Mind - a student is someone who can take those 'punches'.

Did you know?
Wisdom is like the Sun - you rise with it.

Did you know?
You cannot attain Freedom by living freely.

Did you know?
It's unwise to listen to those who say 'it's not what you know it's who you know' – because what you know is the very thing that earns you into the presence of those who know. Therefore

it's not who you know - it's what you know.

Did you know?
Most humans believe that we breathe 'Air' when in fact 'Air breathes us' – so be Free and Follow the Force - do what you Must – just as The Air must... - breathe us...

Did you know?
In emergency combat, if you are faced with someone bigger than you, you should realize that they are slower, louder & heavier, and that you are quicker, quieter & lighter. With that in Mind - you can engage with confidence. What was once seen to be 'advantageous' in your opponent is now seen to be nothing more than a combination of various disadvantages. This truth extends to emergency combat against many as well. It is

possible for one quick, quiet & light combatant to defeat many larger opponents in self-defense - provided a calm & sober state of control & harmony in mind & body is maintained during the encounter.

Did you know?
You cannot help anyone in life until you have first learnt how to help yourself.

Did you know?
All you show is what you know and what you won't... & all you know is what you show and what you don't.

Did you know?
One fundamental for living well is not money but balance because too much of anything is bad; too much food and you will lose agility, too many cigarettes and you will get stale, too much weed and you will become a vegetable, too

much alcohol and you will become an idiot, too much cocaine and you will spaz out, too much water and you will drown, too much earth and you will be buried, too much wind and you will dry up, too much fire and you will burn. So in order to maintain enjoyment of all of life's 'fruits' - exercise self-discipline and revert back to fundamental elements provided by nature and use these as a counter-balance when you party for example. So listen to yourself when you feel like a glass of water or a sandwich while drinking and don't ignore your intuition. Stay mindful and practice discipline like this and you won't gather common problems because as common people we are all happy to get dirty if kept clean for too long and we are all happy to get clean if kept dirty for too long. We are all happy to sleep if kept awake for too long and we are all happy to wake up if kept in slumber for too long. Balance is important for everyone to master no matter who you are or where you come from.

Did you know?
Immoral strength is a weakness & Immoral weakness is a strength.

Did you know?
All insects play the role of 'cleaners' in nature in one way or another. Therefor if you do not wish to have flies, or cockroaches in your home for example, & you also do not enjoy killing them. Then keep your room/place/home clean (all surfaces including yourself) and they will all disappear because they will no longer have any reason to visit... & you will no longer have to feel bad for killing a creature who is just doing their job. It's a win win.

Did you know?
If someone says 'you cannot do that' it literally just means that THEY 'cannot do that' & NOT you. So nod politely but continue on your quest to do what your Soul feels you must... you are onto something others have not yet perceived.

Did you know?
Someone once said - it is us who makes the choice & it is also the choice that makes us.

Did you know?
If you think 'you know something' then you don't know anything - because psychologically speaking - 'The Will To Learn' has been lost or 'put to rest'. & therefor you don't know SHIT on account of your 'Pride' or 'Ego'... because there is always much more to learn from each & every thing.

REJECTED CHAPPIES FACTS

Did you know?
No matter the offense anyone has
caused you - the honour is always
greater in the pardoning of it.

Did you know?
Sediment is 'carried by wind and water'
as the world knows... but it is also
carried and influenced greatly by Light,
Heat & other forms of subtle energy like
Magnetism, just in a much subtler way -
however this is undeclared publicly as
of yet by dictionaries & Scientific
authorities even though expensive
hotels make use of 'indirect-lighting'
which is not only for the comfort of your
vision, but which is also functional in
keeping sediments, chemicals & insects
away from where human beings
congregate between cleaning times.

REJECTED CHAPPIES FACTS

Did you know?

We are the only animals on our home planet who are equipped with Universal and/or Absolute choice yet our animal family members have only so far been granted Relative or Relevant Choice according to their individual natures which are bound by reasons beyond their native understanding for the purposes they must uphold by action within Nature. In other words - you cannot make a squirrel stop collecting nuts and start collecting strawberries, or make a Lion stop living on land and start living under water. But as humans we are able to adapt and adjust accordingly to any environment on our home planet. To wit - one human paradox is a contradiction whereby we are able to change, adapt, adjust & choose any path at any time (there is always a choice) both individually and collectively yet we complain **the most** when any

change becomes a necessary priority
for any further progress in our lives? -
We are able to do anything yet we
convince ourselves and others that we
are not able to do anything, mistaking
the word 'anything' for 'everything' - as
indeed no one can do everything, yet
anyone can do anything. Therefor the
ancient adage of 'if you can change
yourself then you can change the
Universe' remains timeless and stands
strong throughout all the ages. This
saying is of Universal Truth concerning
our beings and the vibratory Universe in
which we are continuously plunged.

Did you know?

You can do anything but if 'your heart'
is not in it don't bother. Find the thing
you love to do and by which time flies
by – that is the thing you must do.

Did you know?
If you can (one day) operate in the world
without any of your actions being at any
negative 'expense' of anyone else, and
by 'negative expense' the meaning
includes emotional, physical & mental
expense and not only financial... Then
you have mastered something called
'individual mastery for communal good'.

Did you know?
The word 'Theory' comes from the
ancient Greek word 'theoria' which
came from an even older Greek word
'theoros' which meant 'to spectate &
contemplate possible meanings and/or
functions of any universal or natural
phenomena'. Theoros meant to 'reach
out and sight-see and experience'. It
was not used in the closed scholarly
manner in which we denote the word
today – 'a supposition or system of
ideas studied in a closed room to

explain something non-present, especially one based on general principles independent of the thing to be explained' – it meant 'to explore, witness, experience & thereafter form an educated reasoning about the phenomena, in order to truly perceive the 'invisible principles' involved'.

Did you know?
Today we use one word to describe a succession of events and a position throughout any calendar known as 'time'. The ancient Greeks however used two words for time; Chronos & Kairos. Chronos meant the mundane succession of seconds, minutes and hours accordingly etc. but Kairos meant the actual unfolding situation in nature &/or society & environment of any given moment; the wind, the trees, the blooming, the state of hills, or the streets etc. The idea of the word Kairos,

traditionally, is known to the wine maker
as an important condition to be aware of
in the process of producing wine. In a
general sense however, the meaning of
Kairos is more apparent within the spirit
of the word 'Seasons' - which in the
same way relates to the actual unfolding
of states of nature &/or anything
(including people) at certain places &
'times'. In other words, in ancient Greek
times, the word 'Kairos' denoted to 'the
depiction of various fluctuating
environmental moments' - 'The Kairos
at 9am was of blooming flowers, singing
birds & fresh air'...

Did you know?
If a church collects donations from a
community but does not use these
donations for public service to any or
even the same community then they are
nothing more than a business exploiting
tax-free donations and the blind faith &

'credulity' of community members as well as the little wages they instead could spare for any charitable cause directly. If this is the case then this fraudulent 'church' should not necessarily be flagged to authorities in law enforcement - as we all know that 99% of authorities in law enforcement don't really do anything even if they claim it (history doesn't lie) but instead members should stop attending immediately & find another spiritually inspiring 'place' – perhaps within themselves? Simple as that.

Did you know?
Heaven helps those who help themselves.

Did you know?
There is a difference in sharing an opinion with others & expecting others to share in your opinion...

REJECTED CHAPPIES FACTS

Did you know?
The higher the society, the lower the morality. Not always but usually...

Did you know?
In the spirit of individual independence & mutual respect for personal freedom - the following words are grasped; 'I can do what I like & you can do what you like but I cannot do what you like if I don't like it because I do not expect you to do what I like if you don't like it'.

Did you know?
If you take a moment to think about what you love... you will find the way within yourself to Utter Appreciation for all the gods, the prophets, the messiahs, and all who have harmonized with God itself and passed examples on of their attunements... Take the time, enjoy the contemplation of the pure

beauty of creation which inspired them - it's worth it.

Did you know?
dafljhsoihgaoirgnnga;lkng;kjnarkgjnlgkn
bjndkjzn,mrfmhafisuncjsda,mdnfref8unn
qfernaklnfreanf499ew9r3010ewkjnfkdjn
flnslanflkansdjfnkjdslanflkjnsdgfkljngkjn
dgkjsankjl. fuk u! (it's important to not take offence and retain a sense of humour)

Did you know?
You are a child of God - meaning you can do whatever you want in good circumstance... do your shit! fuckem all! do your fuckin shit man! Stop procrastinating. Just do it already hoddamit - no need for blood when you got infinite air. beeeatch. Do it - fuck em!

Did you know?
Hope without Action is Undiscovered
Disappointment. Achievement is only
attainable through Action which comes
from the Will which is initiated by the
Mind. Free the Mind - Unleash the Will -
Unveil Extraordinary Abilities...

Did you know?
It is better to be a student of a poor
Master who causes no harm to anyone
else or any other thing - than to be a
slave of someone reckless who
carelessly causes much harm to many
people as well as to many aspects of
Nature itself.

Did you know?
If you wish to attain true discernment,
cease to judge...

Did you know?
A poor person may have no money, no

possessions & no friends as all these are only temporary even if seemingly 'permanent' - yet s/he may have INTEGRITY... A rich person may have money, possessions & many friends but may NOT have integrity. Yet a rich person may have money, possessions & friends as well as INTEGRITY. & a poor person may not only have no money, no possessions, no friends but also no integrity. So never judge a man/woman on their money, possession or how many friends they appear to have. Only judge a person on their INTEGRITY. & you will have discovered a key to true 'discernment'... - As the seemingly 'paradoxical' saying goes - 'if you wish to attain true discernment, cease to judge...' the action of which in itself is a true sign of developed INTEGRITY - which is 'the quality of being honest and having strong moral principles'.

Did you know?
If you perceive the person/people who raised you to be ignorant in one way or another then you have been gifted with the insight to acknowledge that behaviour as ignorant, which means the mind behind all existence has blessed you with a form of Wisdom. So never neglect them in their old age based on their earlier ignorance but rather use your Wisdom to treat them or others like them better in a manner they themselves have not yet discovered.

Did you know?
All beings have Energy on different levels - don't accept or dismiss a person based on their culture, language, sexual preference, religion or skin colour as this is what is known as 'seeing & judging blindly' - rather accept or dismiss a person based on their ENERGY alone... once that is

understood - you will begin to 'see' (feel) something not apparent to our mundane senses...

Did you know?
It is worse to know better and not act - than to not act in ignorance. If it took hardship to gain your knowledge, share your knowledge in actions so that others who see may avoid the hardships you endured - instead of wishing the same hardships on them out of spite & bitterness.

Did you know?
If you have courage to stand up to an abusive person who is causing discomfort to you & others - you will avoid the fault of misdirecting your anger later on to someone else who had nothing to do with it even if they appear to be 'the same'.

Did you know?
The method by which various con-
artists acting as 'motivational speakers'
or 'life coaches' use to get people to
walk over hot coals is no more than a
trick of distracting participants, from the
cold floor they are standing on and the
hot coals they are about to walk over,
by using linguistic influence over their
psychological processes as they pay
attention to the con artist talking to
them. While the con artist fills
participants mind's with all kinds of
motivational jargon they stand bare foot
on a cold surface & the bottom part of
their feet will lower in temperature
naturally (conduction) to a degree cold
enough to allow them to withstand the
high temperature of the coals for a short
time when walking over them... this
leaves participants unharmed with no
pain, blistering or scars to show. This is
no 'miracle', 'magic trick' or 'power of

your mind' in the way the con artist will suggest it to be - it's just nature - temperature fluctuates, pervades and permeates through all matter on Earth 'equassentially' in different degrees constantly thanks to the Sun & the Moon. When you are cold you counter act your state with heat to stop yourself from getting colder, when you are hot you counter act your state with cold to stop yourself from getting hotter, to whatever extreme, it is true that if you heat yourself up **before** you go into the cold you can avoid the cold momentarily, and if you cool yourself down **before** you go into the heat you can avoid the heat momentarily, and vice versa in many different ways possible in the light of the Universe, or God's application of Good Balance for Health in All nature. If you place your hand in a bowl of freezing cold water with ice, once the hand or portion of the body becomes very cold, you may run a small amount of boiling water (one teaspoon) over the very cold skin and not burn, blister or scar. We're warm blooded – meaning blood congregates where it's warm, so if you have made the area cold which has caused the blood to withdraw from the surface area, meaning no blood is in contact with surface skin to transmit electrical signals to your brain to sound the alarm of 'this is too hot!'. Then when you momentarily touch something so hot that, at room temp, would usually burn the shit out of you, in this state of 'temporary anesthetic' you will avoid the burn, blister and scar. This is one way to succeed in 'fooling your sense of touch'. Maybe that's a bit extreme for everyone to try but then simply try this experiment... the next time you have a hot meal or pie or whatever food as long as it's very hot, get yourself a cold drink

– very cold. Take a gulp of your very cold cold drink (preferably with ice) first and when you can feel your lips and mouth are very cold - immediately take a small bite of your piping hot food which would usually burn your lips – you will not burn. If you tried to eat that same bite at normal temperature – you would burn. This knowledge should never be used to fool anyone else for fun or for profitable gain but rather for the maintenance of good health for yourself. After the latter experience is experienced a brief or lengthy meditation on the law involved will serve to enlighten the individual in many ways concerning some of the purposes of The Moon & The Sun & the effects thereof (seasons) and which will in effect serve you well to avoid much physical pain. We live in a world where the trend is to withhold knowledge and 'cure people of ailments for a price'

REJECTED CHAPPIES FACTS

rather than to provide knowledge to people in order for them to 'prevent themselves from ailments for free'. Not only are these con artists misleading innocent people with the knowledge they have attained by exploiting it instead of passing it on - during the elated moment of achievement on the part of the unknowing participants (after they have succeeded in walking over the coals unharmed in a state of amazement not knowing how it was truly achieved) - the con artist will then immediately motivate all of them to buy his or her over-priced book full of nonsense, buy into his or her online course with no real point, buy tickets to his or her next 'special convention/event', or any other bullshit he or she can come up with to exploit your hard earned incomes. So don't be fooled by those encouraging your superstition just to get your money but secure yourself by searching for Truth and use that Truth for the betterment of your own life & in effect the lives of others - you have the right to question anything & everything. **This should only be used by and for Adults only** & I pass this knowledge on mainly to help the poor Adults around who wish to keep good health to help themselves when no one else will. The skill may be used to remove warts or infections by burning them off without pain or the need of injected alcohol (which is expensive). The success of removing a surface ailment is achievable without pain simply by applying this knowledge of using extreme cold first before applying something hot like a soldering iron to a wart for example – and no pain will be felt if done correctly. The extreme cold temperature will act to momentarily numb the infected surface area by repelling the warm blood away

from under the surface 'fooling the
sense of touch in that area' and a
common instrument such as a soldering
iron may be used to burn off a wart or
any other skin infection (you must cool
the infected skin area until the cold is no
longer bearable – then apply extreme
heat for a few seconds at a time only).
Make sure to have a bandage or plaster
with anti-septic ready to cover the
wound once the procedure is complete
– this can be obtained at much lower
costs as compared to going to a medical
clinic. If you feel burning pain then you
are rushing – re-apply the ice to the
infected area immediately and try again.
The same goes for using freezing water
and boiling water to sterilize & sanitize
dirty surfaces within the home without
harming the wood or metals if
performed correctly – for a cleaner
environment that promotes health
instead of the opposite and yet in many

cases – without any soap at all. This also applies to pulled muscles that are 'tightly held by cold' – apply a hot or warm object such as a 'hot water bottle' to the painful muscle and you will feel a lot better after several minutes as 'heat handles all matter, serving to untangle, and cold holds all matter, serving to tighten'. It's dangerous to 'play with fire' so be very careful & aware & only test it on yourself – do not test on others – but understand that it is impossible 'to fight fire with fire' & if you succeed in finding the true answer as to 'how to fight fire' – then you will indeed – be able to 'walk on fire'.

Did you know?
The phrase 'look after yourself' does not mean 'take care of yourself' as it is often used. 'Take care of yourself' means take care of yourself. 'Look after

yourself' means 'observe, or be aware of, what your actions leave behind you'.

Did you know?
An enlightened person once said - The word 'Love' is a synonym for the word 'Life'. Therefor the more full of Love a person is the more full of Life they are as well.

Did you know?
Children are not only there for adults to teach – they are also there for adults to learn from.

Did you know?
The phrase 'Father, forgive them they know not what they do' does not necessarily mean to 'pardon a person or people mercifully because they don't know what they are doing' as it is widely believed today. The latter is still a plausible interpretation, as

people perceive it, denoting to the statement. It is good to pardon trespassers as soon as possible. But it is also strongly arguable that the original intention of the words uttered meant to 'Give-Before, or, to Pre-Give of yourself, your knowledge (or anything of use) to anyone (when or if) they don't know what to do'. In terms of the possible etymology of the word 'forgive'. This possibility changes things and is a 'more wonderful' interpretation for several reasons. Firstly it's aimed at the conscience of everyone because everyone knows something for the good of others & to do so when those others need it and don't know what to do is a great act which unveils honest gratitude from the person receiving – & it always stimulates a great feeling of love within the person giving as well. All of us in one way or another have needs that we cannot provide for ourselves, the knowledge of a good doctor, electrician, plumber, admin clerk, teacher or anyone - when these practitioner's expertise are correctly applied or passed on for someone in need (who does not know what to do) it is always a true blessing as we can all agree... therefor it is arguable that the aforementioned famous phrase was intended as 'one last inspiring instruction' or statement to embody the principle which can be phrased in different words as 'to give when someone is in need (and does not know what to do) because that is what the creator has done', instead of the phrase being used in the spirit of 'pardon them because they do not know what they are doing' – as (for more reasons) this current interpretation risks prolonging ignorance on the one hand instead of the interpretation of applying attained 'know-how' to those who don't know on the other. The current interpretation also risks cultivating 'elitism' instead of equal-importance of all. Equal-importance being the essence embodied in this proposed interpretation because it doesn't put the 'knower' in an 'elite position', but in a position of servitude to others which is the purpose of attaining knowledge in the first place because all living beings are equally important even if less capable in different ways. No one person is more important than another no matter their education, race, sex or beliefs. Obviously concerning certain things a person may be more advanced at something than another person, but in the grand

scheme of things no one is more
important than another. So in the light
of these reasons it is very possible
that the interpretation put forth herein
was in fact the original and former
intention of the phrase and that over
time the meaning of the phrase has
been degraded to an ignorant
interpretation, the use of which is
subtly conducive to control for few
instead of freedom for all. So it seems
very plausible that the original
statement has lost it's original
meaning today. Everyone knows
something which can be of benefit to
another, and that is as true today as it
was thousands of years ago, and as
true as it will be in thousands of years
to come. It's an Immortal Universal
Fact. So in a nutshell the
interpretation - 'to pre-give when you
can see that someone is in need (and

does not know what to do)'
encourages Mutual Obligation, Love &
Togetherness while 'pardon them
because they don't know what they
are doing' indoctrinates Elitism, Hate
& Division. But for further reasoning
the proposed interpretation put forth
herein of the meaning of the
statement seems more plausible
because as we all know – the person
who made the statement was against
elitism and went against a dominion of
control, hate & division armed with
Freedom, Love & Divine
Understanding right until the end even
during his suffering. This master
avatar 'forgave/pre-gave/gave before'
his example and knowledge not
known, or forgotten, by the human
inhabitants of the time as a 'further
understanding' or a 'reminiscent
reminder' in order to help people help

themselves and likewise many others down the ages who have found the being's teachings helpful. His intention was not to 'pardon the ignorant & leave them hanging with no solution' as the current interpretation suggests. His intention was to, by example, help others lift themselves up out of suffering, an example which served as a reminder, during a dark time, of the driving force of all life – which is Love – this is the true driving force behind life & all important aspects of life, such as all true knowledge and abilities that serve to raise a person and others out of a less enjoyable existence. Love runs the show of life & in the name of Love we should all pre-give of ourselves when we feel the 'inner nudge' to do something if we see someone is struggling. Try it - it feels great, & it also accomplishes greatness. If we think about this interpretation long enough it begins to resonate and 'ring true' within ourselves which in-turn provides us with a more wonderful disposition concerning life.

Did you know?
All musical notes, keys & sounds do possess healing power through the vibrations they emit.

Did you know?
A suicidal person does not wish to die, they simply wish to no longer live as a slave to another person or persons, or to bare the weight of mistakes made by others which they are innocent of but which others have immediately blamed them for because they themselves, through ignorance, did not wish to seek the true cause of a matter or take responsibility for their own fault. This is

the human cruelty we all know too well. As an example - No one should immediately blame someone for breaking a 20 year old wooden stool by mistake - without accounting for natural depreciation. That's not to say that a person cannot be reckless and break something purposefully out of jealousy or some childish trait, but in some cases it's more likely that the age of the something broken made it more susceptible to break which often goes unnoticed by covetous people. So as an analogy – a cleaner who didn't mean to break something but who's only income comes from cleaning the house of a covetous person who hoards possessions may eventually, after countless false accusations, adopt a depression which eventually may lead to the entertainment of suicidal thoughts. So usually motivation in the spirit of welcoming the honest thoughts of the suicidal person (to speak their true thoughts) can free them from a state of suicidal tendencies, because their thoughts are usually true and may resonate with others and serve to find a hidden solution to a problem, which reminds them that they live for a reason and an important purpose.

Did you know?
The word 'drug' originally meant 'any substance that has an action on the body' – this includes salt, sugar and even herbs. Since too much of any drug can be adverse on the host – in the long run it would greatly benefit any person to enjoy as little as possible instead of as much as possible. Less, if at all possible, 'is more' for better health in the case of drug influence.

Did you know?
Money in itself doesn't solve anything
unless used as a tool in a Frugal &
Priority-driven manner. 'Frugal
Functionality' is key to staying out of
debt. Chasing money doesn't achieve
anything except an understanding of
how dangerous stress levels can arise.
Money misused can be detrimental to
any home or person, but money used
responsibly and appropriately can aid to
the advancement of the same. Either
way the choice of use of money in fact
has nothing to do with money itself at
all, or how much you have of it, but the
understanding applied to it is the key as
it is just a tool created for use, not a
trophy to brag about or flaunt to others.
Money gives freedom of use allowing

you to choose to use it for anything you want. But knowing that what you want is different to what you need enlightens you. If you need something you alone must choose the thing you need most and not let others influence you to misuse your hard-earned money for what they think you need unless, after careful investigation, it makes sense. If it doesn't then disregard the ignorant advice. No one can know what is truly needed for someone else but the person in need, which is a human fact, and that is why we have human rights. It's your right to not act on impulse according to another person's command. If someone tries to urge you to act on impulse, and you are not sure what to do, don't do anything... – until you are sure of what needs to be done – & then act immediately on your own accord. The first thing you need 'to get' in order to be successful in the use of money as a

tool is not money at all, but
understanding.


Did you know?
If you pray for God or anyone else to do
something for you which you yourself
are capable of (only you can know) then
you are not cultivating faith but you are
cultivating laziness and error.

Did you know?
Prayer should only be ascribed to giving
thanks, asking for an answer or an
instruction only. It is still up to you to
act on it if it is received.

Did you know?
Live, Love, Accept, 'Pre-Give', & you will
see Perfection & understand the true
meaning of the word 'Faith'.

Did you know?

We all know how to dress appropriately for dates, weddings, church, school or work, but one thing no one is ever taught is how to dress appropriately for walking the streets... If you don't have a car & need to walk the streets, dress down, wear old clothes that will cover you up simply and appropriately. There's no need to be dirty (old clothes can be clean), but there is definitely no need to be 'flashy' either. In this way you will avoid criminals and predators preying on those who naively believe that nothing bad can happen to them no matter what they do or how they dress. You can avoid trouble without the need to fight or even break a sweat just by simply dressing down and leaving your phone and wallet at home and only taking the amount of notes you need or just your card in your pocket - when you have to walk the streets to, for example, get something from the shops. Be

comfortable without drawing attention –
but appear to have nothing and no one
will want anything from you...

Did you know?
If a person is wrought with hate it is not
enjoyable for them. So if you accept
them with understanding (knowing that
you have no idea what they have been
through in life) – you will be of a much
greater help to that person if you apply
that Love & understanding by simply not
taking offence – instead of wasting
precious energy by reacting to their
hate with more hate.

Did you know?
A false politician is a puppet who tells
stories to hide the truth of an event or
situation. A true artist is a master who
tells stories to unveil the Truth of an
event or situation. Often the politician
has a selfish intention with a hidden

agenda and an attitude of being 'more important than others' - which is a problem that serves as 'A Wall to Freedom'. A true artist often possesses a selfless intention and an attitude of 'less-importance to others' – & who's actions nevertheless always seem to act towards the propounding of a solution toward an allegorical 'Bridge to Freedom'.

Did you know?
You do not necessarily get what is fair in life, but you get what you can Endure. If you can't endure it – don't accept it. If you can endure it you will bare it without blinking.

Did you know?
Although we don't know enough about gravity to master it accept a few adept beings who have mastered levitation – we still know WHY it is necessary in the

Universe because of the result we live in. And if it were non-existent we, and our planet, and the Moon & the Sun and all other forms, would not even be portions of tiny congregated particles either... as some do state that 'if gravity did not exist we would all be dispersed as particles' - but even more than that – matter would be of such an infinitely dispersed 'matter' that an 'imaginary observer' could argue that nothing would even reach the state of being an observable particle in the first place.

Did you know?
The best 'hiding' you can give an abusive person, commonly known as a bully, isn't laying a finger on them at all, but instead - exposing them and letting shame do the rest. It takes the least energy and is still the most effective method. & If you do not give this 'adequate hiding' to an abusive person,

or a 'bully'... they will think they can keep getting away with their abuse & continue to abuse many more... & the older the bully gets without having been disciplined in the first place - the harder 'the hiding' should naturally be - through the act of exposure.

Did you know?
If a person keeps coming back to the same problem in their life – it usually means they have not learnt the lesson the mind behind it all is trying to impart to them completely yet. Be grateful, and pay attention to every lesson thoroughly to save yourself much frustration.

Did you know?
In all the writings of all ancient scriptures – it is an attempt to try and explain something that cannot be reached by mere words... therefor – don't only read what was written but

rather try to read what was 'trying to be written'.


Did you know?
Deep & completely private meditation may lead to an expanse of 'mental freedom' (freeing the Soul from the body) which can interfere with radio and electro-magnetic waves... provided the student pays absolutely no attention to their material surroundings but instead focuses on lofty ideas such as the question of eternity.

Did you know?
Many people mistake moral weakness for strength – to their detriment and the detriment of others. Sadly.

Did you know?
Immoral strength is a weakness & Immoral weakness is a strength.


REJECTED CHAPPIES FACTS

Did you know?
Slate rock is formed naturally from sand
and weather without the need for money
- after the heat has loosened all
surface-sand into many small
susceptible parts, the rain and cold of a
storm serves to suppress or 'arrest'
(cold) the loose sand & compress (rain)
the sand into 'slate rocks' naturally.
More or less – the same principle is
used industrially to turn sand into stone
for the benefit of building homes &/or
various shelters made of rock as rock is
indeed a concentrated form of 'slate' or,
compressed sands...

Did you know?
Nothing hurts like emotional pain – you
can be the toughest motherfucker in
this world and emotional pain will still
wipe you out.

REJECTED CHAPPIES FACTS

Did you know?
Depression is the cause of all premature
debilitation. Stay Positive – don't let
negativity in.

Did you know?
You must use your knowledge to feel as
good & vital as the movements of all
things in Nature – just as you must use
yourself to do or make something useful
in order to feel good about yourself.

Did you know?
When someone forces you into a
situation and you have a feeling that
something is wrong – you are right to
pay attention to that feeling - & you
must immediately act on it to get
yourself out of that situation – do not
hesitate no matter what anyone says &
even if you appear to be 'mad' &/or if
you cannot explain yourself – most
words cannot describe feelings in any

case so don't waste your time. & Do not
attempt to appeal to the person's better
nature or understanding as they may
very well not have cultivated this
throughout their life and therefor you
will find it to be unavailable. Once you
are free from the situation – do not let
these experiences make you bitter or
angry, don't allow any space in your
heart for hate – rather continue to
maintain and cultivate your own better
nature for your own life. The only
person we can manage &/or change is
ourselves.

Did you know?
As long as you entertain and succumb
to the coercions of others - you will
never be truly happy.

Did you know?
If you take someone's life – you will
never enjoy your own again. Just

observe any killer in a jail cell – they're not having a good time even if they are pretending to. So never believe those who claim that there is nothing wrong with killing.

Did you know?
Medication is never a cure and you don't need it except for in an emergency - it can stimulate certain immune functions or it can alleviate pain while the body naturally heals itself from an injury or ailment, but it doesn't cure you & in most cases it will make you docile, sedated, numb & dumb. So it should only ever be used if all natural solutions have been exhausted. Understand – it is a drug and the abuse of it can be argued to be just as bad as the abuse of any unregulated drug. It's effects are more subtle and creep up over a longer period of time, but once it fucks you you're fucked all the same. How can we

be expected to applaud a world where there are billions of prescription-drug-addicts today and it's encouraged commercially? And when a completely healthy person who practices natural healthy activities is criticized as having 'something wrong with them' when they refuse medication for a small injury or even just a headache - how can that be right? If you continue to resort to meds immediately each time – you will continue to mask the cause of the problem, the discovery of which would provide the solution to natural prevention instead of resorting to a fake 'cure' for that particular problem time & time again.

Did you know?
Anything in moderation is less of a threat to your health & too much of anything is more of a threat to your health.

REJECTED CHAPPIES FACTS

Did you know?
When you get mad you feel bad you get
sad, repeat that... until you see that you
need that to be glad to leave that – in
your Mind. The choice has always, and
will always be, yours alone.

Did you know?
If you have a desire to maintain natural
health without all the medication people
have become accustomed to
constantly... besides habitually drinking
clean water - you must also master
eating & sleeping well (not abundantly,
but balanced). You cannot sleep well if
you have not been active well, you
cannot eat well (or keep a healthy
appetite) unless you are active enough
& sleep enough, you cannot eat well if
you cannot shit well either. And you

cannot shit well unless you eat well, sleep well &/or be active well. You cannot eat well, sleep well, shit well, or confidently get active well - unless you **keep clean well**. You cannot (have the energy or ability to) clean well unless you eat well, which cannot happen if you don't shit well, which cannot happen unless you sleep well. In fact none of these five attributes can be achieved if the others are not present – they co-operate. So only eat when you're hungry and stop when you're full. Cleaning in itself is probably the wisest of all activities anyone can cultivate for themselves to have a healthy life. Not only is it a good work out, it saves you money from not going to a gym and not hiring a cleaner, it makes your place enjoyable for you to spend time in peacefully. Depending on the size of your room, flat or home - it shouldn't take more than a few minutes a morning to maintain and there is no need for anyone else to do it but yourself. The same goes for making your own food – it saves and can help you avoid getting sick because you are observing that the food is well cooked over the entire process instead of relying on the unspoken promise of someone else. But most important - you cannot do any of the above unless your mental state is calm and peaceful, to which the irony is attached that the above activities are, as a matter of fact, very instrumental and conducive to a peaceful mind. Cleaning is not simply applying soap and water, that's a good start, but you also need to air out the room and it's best to use the day for this, in other words – clean when the sun is out instead of at night – because all microscopic particles follow the heat & light, so its more effective when there's sunlight than cleaning at night when there is far less outside-light and far more inside-light. Have you ever noticed how scents/smells, smoke fumes & dust particles linger around lights and warmer areas of any place? You can also use hot water to rinse surfaces that still smell of the chemicals from the soaps used (if you cannot see soap or dirt but can still smell them then they are still there and will decay & you will inhale those decaying chemicals in small doses over time whether you realize it or not, even when some people get a blocked nose they don't seem to 'join the dots' and always say 'I don't know why' but they still continue to leave chemicals everywhere – which go airborne and are inhaled), anyways - then lastly go over the now heated clean surface with cold water to bring the surface temperature of the surfaces **below** room temperature. A clean lower temperature object than the room temp repels bacteria from that surfaces and out the aerated room toward the light because most bacteria follows warmth and they also gather where there is a combination of decaying matter and moderate temperature – being near to that combination will make a person more susceptible to sickness by means of inhalation, but having the opposite condition – by 'sealing' the cleaning session with low temperature after 'heat-rinsing' is a cheap & very strong fortitude for avoiding sickness and maintaining vitality. You can then let the room heat up again naturally and you will notice a pleasant natural healthy scent appear without chemicals – or the use of air fresheners. Generally speaking keeping a room cool in a warm climate may be achieved cheaply just by promoting shade or – leaving lights off or as low as possible during the day which also saves your income. This can keep a room cool without expensive air conditioning. Likewise in a cold climate, heat can be achieved by the culmination of a simple light bulb over time with windows and doors shut for a time, the same goes for a simple candle or even just body heat as it expels it's energy into the immediate environment & over time, it contributes to warming up the place. Patience is necessary to notice these advantages without the need to spend money or get medication – in an attempt to unveil strong fortitudes against an unhealthy living space. It is achievable, in fact, without money or medication – but it is only achievable by being in a state of mind that is utterly Peaceful. Another near-free method to maintain good health is to practice the habit of having a glass of pure water after every intake of food or flavoured drink. Why? - consider that all food, flavoured liquids like fizzy drinks and anything else you can 'eat' even sweets all begin to decay much quicker when exposed in small amounts or 'sediments' (like left over crumbs on a plate or pieces stuck in your teeth) & more than this - they begin, if not consumed, to decay & fester in warm containers in a concentrated way as it's less possible for the decaying and septic fumes to escape the container (we've all forgotten a sandwich in a lunch box at some point and opened the container too late to smell toxic fumes and find a decaying sandwich). Now – understand that your mouth is a container. Even if you could carry a toothbrush around with you all the time a better solution is – if you simply have a small drink of clean water after every meal or coffee or after any 'foods' – **before** the taste starts to turn sour (yes you will sacrifice the lingering taste you're enjoying, but you are controlling

your sense of taste instead of being
controlled by it & you are also leaving
nothing to chance in terms of small
amounts of food or sugary drinks (as all
consumables even drinks do decay) left
in thin amounts to decay in your mouth
(a near-free prevention of illness) & you
are also disciplining yourself to not
over-eat as lingering tastes stimulate
'false hunger' unnecessary in terms of
'needed consumption'. At that point you
don't actually need more food, you just
think you need more when you actually
are fooled into thinking you need to
taste something else before the taste in
your mouth goes bad because you don't
know any other way to 'fix it', but you
can master this by clearing all taste
completely with simple pure drinking
water before it gets to that point – try it
because it's completely healthy & free
and you will notice that your focus on
food leaves you and you are then able

to direct your attention to other activities like reading, writing, walking, thinking, singing, creating etc. You will also send the last bits of food in tiny amounts down to a part of your digestive system more capable of managing waste than your sometimes sealed, sometimes half-open warm container (your mouth) and you will have successfully avoided the risk of exposure to decaying left overs – the direct and concentrated inhalation of which will definitely make you feel unwell. Those decaying bits are the direct cause of a 'stinky morning mouth/breath' which is cleared significantly by simply drinking water after eating – brushing your teeth aside. The same goes for the sediment left by smoking. Prevent much of it all together with water rather than having to endure it later. We make ourselves sick, flu isn't 'the colds fault' as people assume, it's actually a combination of dirt in the form of minute decaying particles (from chemicals to food or drink) being inhaled in containers (even your room is a container) and at the same time not counter balancing our state of hot/cold with the appropriate opposite end of temperature sufficiently in balance to maintain comfort. This is why meditation is so good for anyone to help them get back on track if they have let their environment get too 'out of hand' from the simple, manageable & peaceful ideal they had for themselves to begin with. There's no need to sit like a Buddha statue with legs folded when meditating and there's no need to spend money to 'learn how to meditate' – it's not a group activity but it's an ability which can only be achieved alone.  You can meditate in any position – it's simply the practice of clearing your Mind in order to think more clearly and to behave more constructively. Thoughts rush in when we try to calm our mind, so a great help is to focus on something beautiful, something you love, something inspiring - and to tell all other thoughts to, basically, 'fuck off'. You need to neglect all unwanted thoughts. You will, after some practice, realize that you are in a far more peaceful & enjoyable state of mind. & naturally as your mind clears – you find it easier and simple to clean your lodging as well. This Peace of Mind will contribute towards a healthy balance of the aforementioned five processes (sufficient action, sufficient sleep, cleaning, eating & shitting well) and what's more – everything else enjoyable will follow from these. But an **understanding** of the need of cleanliness and a balanced healthy bodily 'intake' (eat), 'out-take' (shit), 'use of energy' (action) & 'regaining of energy' (sleep) is very necessary in order to create a healthy existence. To someone who truly understands - these five processes become the prioritized 'orders of the day' for a peaceful mind because they co-operate. One cannot be achieved without the other, but none can be achieved without a peaceful state of mind. Therefor Peace Of Mind should be the most prioritized goal or Ideal for anyone who wants to achieve a healthy life without the constant need for medication. & A 'Peaceful Outlook' usually goes hand-in-hand with a Loving outlook! So keep to the positives of everything – Joy, Peace, Love, Kindness, Compassion etc.

Did you know?
It is possible to be healthy without medication, knowledgeable without education & rich without money. The answers to the questions that may arise from these statements have been

hidden where they have always been
hidden since your life began – deep
within yourself.

Did you know?
One of the biggest misconceptions
anyone can make is to confuse a silent
person for a stupid person - the
complete opposite is true.

Did you know?
Money is not a metric for love, it's not a
measure for success, & it's not the
make of mastery.

Did you know?
When people boast about knowing
something but cannot explain it or
demonstrate it then they don't know
what they're talking about. The proof is
in the very fact that they are still talking
and not yet 'walking'. As you learn - you
must apply the knowledge you are

attaining until you can truly demonstrate what you know so that you can establish your stride as someone 'mastered in a craft'...

Did you know?
You don't have to impress anyone, be validated by anyone, seek approval from anyone, get consensus from anyone – if you have discovered the Truth about yourself.

Did you know?
Master 'not wasting' and you will master 'not needing'.

Did you know?
Wash your dishes immediately after meals and your health will improve rapidly.

Did you know?
There are traces of sophisticated
technologies that existed millennia BC.
Such as ancient runways the world
over... as well as ancient hieroglyphs
that depict airplanes and helicopters.

Did you know?
The oldest computer in the world was
found in a sunken ship off the coast of
Greece not long ago & is speculated to
being at least two thousand years old
with accurate monitoring of the planets
in our solar system.

Did you know?
The educational system is only
approximately 350 years old. Before
then people traditionally acquired
knowledge by apprenticing with a
master of a craft that a student wished

REJECTED CHAPPIES FACTS

to learn from. In countless modern cases many successful people today still claim to have only acquired worthwhile know-how in this manner alone.

Did you know?
Concerning 'the idea of a master' - A real master does not choose students, the student chooses the master – understanding that a master is not someone who has control over many – it is someone who has mastered themselves alone.

Did you know?
It remains a mystery as to why so many people still believe or accept a president as someone with actual knowledge & ability for the benefit of the people. So few of them have demonstrated actual effective improvement for the people but so many of them have proven to be

nothing more than con artists time &
time again (despite all their efforts to
convince you of their validity in words –
while lacking much in action). More than
that – the worst of them always serve
the longest terms because they don't
know what they are doing - while the
few (best of them) honoured all their
commitments over short terms because
they knew exactly what they were
doing. Don't believe propaganda hype
designed to 'milk your attention' –
propaganda hype is usually bigger when
they want to take your focus off matters
they don't want to be responsible for
when they should be as 'responsible
leaders' - because they don't know
what they're doing but admitting that
would lose your vote and their
excessive incomes.

Did you know?

When you have a thought and a will to do something but then put it off until later - the thought returns with a feeling of annoyance because action was not taken in the first place. But when you know what should be done & you do it immediately - you never need to worry about it again.

Did you know?
From life comes death & from death comes life because in Nature there is no 'death'. So don't worry you can live peacefully knowing that this existence is eternal even if it doesn't appear that way.

Did you know?
Nature doesn't make mistakes – people do.

Did you know?

REJECTED CHAPPIES FACTS

God doesn't need us - we need God.
End of story.

Did you know?
It will benefit you greatly to judge a
person on their actions rather than what
they say.

Did you know?
The Art of Writing is in itself an Action
and must not be confused with cheap
talk.

Did you know?
The Moon & The Sun will never collide –
the two are physically separate but they
are as One in Purpose.

Did you know?
The most important things in life cannot
be seen with the physical eyes. These

REJECTED CHAPPIES FACTS

can only observe the least important things.

Did you know?
Balance is as a bow & arrow – if pulled past the threshold of 'the point of ease' – it is found to have force yet the arrow misses it's target...

Did you know?
The differences in people are unimportant and focusing on them never did any good. But the things people share in common are most important and focusing on them has always brought about much good.

Did you know?
If you ever find yourself 'in the shit' then be calm, make a plan – & apply it.

Did you know?
If someone claims 'life will end' you
should not believe them. Life is eternal.
Planets may end but life will always
carry on in one way or another.

Did you know?
Human beings have lived on this planet
for millions of years. There's no need to
believe the fear-induction of complete
human demise. Nor do you need to
believe people who claim the world will
end on a specific date or time. Over the
last century there have been countless
claims like this and not one of them
have come true.

Did you know?
The 'End Of The World' or Apocalypse
does not mean Earth & all existence,
human included, will end – it just means
that human habits will need to change in
preparation to survive the adaptation of

the earth's cyclical adjustments it
makes every 26,000 years.


Did you know?
Saying goodbye to a faulty past is not
an end but a welcoming of a new future.

Did you know?
If you master the practice of relying
solely on your sense of smell when
cooking food – you will never need to
follow written instructions again.

Did you know?
The closer to death we come the more
we see what life is all about.

Did you know?
Only city people claim that the whole
world is over populated. Only single
people encourage others to break up

REJECTED CHAPPIES FACTS

with their loved one. Only jobless people encourage others to quit their jobs.

Did you know?
Salt is something you sometimes cannot live with & sometimes cannot live without.

Did you know?
If you disallow self-discipline then you are deluded by the debilitation of your decadence.

Did you know?
If reincarnation is true it would help explain the phenomenon of prodigy children & many people who possess knowledge & abilities which were not taught to them in this lifetime.

Did you know?

A person who ages well naturally understands the balance of things so well that you may overhear them make statements such as 'in hot climates it's best to simply be in the shade & in cold climates it's best to simply be in the Sun whenever possible'... & 'In Winter it's best to eat warm foods, in Summer it's best to eat cold foods' etc.

Did you know?
If you get a feeling followed by a thought of someone before they call or surprise-visit you – then you have an ability which, if you explored further, would greatly benefit you in life.

Did you know?
Any ability only becomes perfected by practice. There is no such thing as 'raw talent' – only practice until something is mastered.

Did you know?
The meaning of the word 'Practical' is
'of or concerned with the actual doing
or use of something rather than with
theory or ideas'. It comes from the Old
French word 'practique', via the late
Latin word (from Greek) 'praktikos'
meaning 'concerned with action', from
'prattein' meaning to 'do, act' but it also
comes from the latest archaic word
before it's existence 'practic' which you
will notice is only one letter away from
the modern word 'PRACTICE'!!!

Did you know?
There is no end.

REJECTED CHAPPIES FACTS

REJECTED CHAPPIES FACTS